# THE THREE SPHERES OF GLORY

## A Compilation

BIBLE STUDENT'S PRESS ™
*Windber, Pennsylvania*

***The Three Spheres of Glory:*** *A Compilation*
Copyright © 2018 by Bible Student's Press™
All rights reserved.


Executive Editor: André Sneidar
Layout and Design: Great Adventure in Faith
Compilation Series Editor: Mark Peters
Cover design by Nathan Hyde Pilkington


    ISBN:     978-1-62904-281-7

Published by:
Bible Student's Press™
An imprint of *Pilkington & Sons*
  P.O. Box 265
  Windber, PA 15963
  1-800-784-6010

For information on *Bible Student's Press*™ releases, visit
   *www.BibleStudentsPress.com*

For information on other Bible study resources, visit
   *www.StudyShelf.com*

*Printed in the United States of America.*

Dr. E. W. Bullinger (1837-1913)

Henry W. Fry (1848-1939)

Charles H. Welch (1880-1967)

# Contents

1. The Three Spheres: Distinguishing Between Them ...................9
2. Three Spheres of Glory ............................................................. 13
3. The Three Spheres ......................................................................23
4. The Hope of the Third Sphere ...................................................43
5. The 3 Dispensational "Hopes" of the 3 Spheres of Glory ......... 51

# Chapter 1

## The Three Spheres: Distinguishing Between Them

*by* — H.W. Fry

When we set ourselves to study the Scriptures, we should especially acquaint ourselves with the deep things of God, such as the *"Mystery"* spoken of by Paul in Ephesians 3:4.

It is important, for instance, to note that God's calling relates to three distinct *spheres*: an Earthly sphere; a second, Heavenly (or spiritual) sphere; and a third or still more exalted sphere, which is called by the Apostle Paul, the *"On-High Calling"*[1] (Philippians 3:14).

### THE FIRST SPHERE:
*Earthly*

The Earthly sphere encompasses the *first* Covenant with Abraham, where God gave him the Land of Palestine, and he was to be the father of a mighty nation, with earth-seed like unto the sand of the sea (Genesis 22:17). This earthly kingdom was entirely temporal, centered on the nation Israel. In Moses' day the Law was added to this Earthly Sphere.

### THE SECOND SPHERE:
*Heavenly*

The Heavenly (or spiritual) sphere is represented by God's *second* covenant with Abraham. Some thirty years after the first covenant God promised

---

1. [*Editor*] "*High*" is the Greek adverb ἄνω (*anō*) meaning "up," "upward, or on the top" (Strong's), *i.e.*, *"the upward calling"* (Rotherham).
    This is the "sphere of glory *'where Christ sitteth at the right hand of God'* (Colossians 3:1,2) ... the third and highest sphere of blessing ... This third sphere of blessing is said to be *'far above all principality and power' 'in the super-heavenlies'* (Ephesians 1:20,21)." – Charles Welch, "Above," *Alphabetical Analysis*

Abraham another seed, a heavenly-seed, likened this time to the stars of heaven.

This seed was to be spiritual, and was to include all of those of *"many nations"* who would believe God as Abraham did. Abraham was thus to be the father of the faithful. This was not a temporal seed or kingdom, but was entirely spiritual, or heavenly, encompassing an election out of Israel and the *"many nations."* It was to culminate in the new or Heavenly Jerusalem, the *"city whose Builder and Maker is God"* Himself (Hebrews 11:10).

Abraham and the elect from Israel and the *"many nations"* inherit this city as *"the Bride, the Lamb's wife."* When this Covenant was made its sphere was much higher than the Earthly, though it would run concurrent with it. The first sphere was Earthly, while this second sphere was Heavenly.

## THE THIRD SPHERE:
*Far Above All Heavens*

When the Earthly and Heavenly Spheres were rejected by the Jews, God authorized Paul to proclaim a new calling, the *"Mystery,"* with its accompanying new sphere. This sphere was vastly higher than the previous spheres.

After Israel was declared Lo-ammi[2] (Hosea 1:9), God not merely extended His grace, but revealed the *"exceeding riches of His Grace"* (Ephesians 2:7), which exposed a far grander sphere – the *"On-High Calling"* (Philippians 3:14). This calling does not culminate in the Heavenly Jerusalem which comes down to earth, but up into a sphere that is *"far above all heavens"* (Ephesians 4:10). This is the sphere of *"the Church,[3] which is His Body"* (Ephesians 1:22-23).

The majority of this day, if they have any definite ideas on the subject, prob-

---

2. Israel was not to be rejected without ample warning, and so God in His mercy specially endued the Apostles with spiritual gifts and great powers, by which they could show great *"signs and wonders,"* in order to prove that they were messengers sent by God. But notwithstanding these signs of tongues, healing, etc., the nation was stubborn in their rejection of Christ, until Paul was finally authorized to declare their rejection by God, as narrated in Acts 28:25-28.

3. [*Editor:*] The Greek word often translated as *"church"* in most English versions is ἐκκλησία (*ekklēsia,* or ecclesia). The word is a compound word meaning "called-out" (*ek* = "out"; *kaleō* = called). The ecclesia is God's "called-out" ones. The ecclesia is not a building or denomination; not a meeting, or doctrinal creed; it is not somewhere we go, or something we do, it is who we as believers *are*.

ably consider the new Jerusalem as their future home, where they will be gathered as *"the Bride"* (Revelation 21:9), and this is precisely what the Old Testament saints expected (Hebrews 11:10). This is true of all who are *"born again"* as were the Old Testament saints when they kept the Law and thus obeyed God, and were not *"cut off"* (Exodus 12:15) from their privileges.

However, the distinctive privilege of the present is that an elect are called, through the Sovereign Will of God, to an inheritance in the third sphere of which very little is generally known, but which ought to be our special study.

The thorough comprehension of the relative importance of each of these spheres will greatly assist in *"rightly dividing the Word of Truth."* It is worth a great effort and every careful attention in order to have this knowledge always available.

# Chapter 2
## Three Spheres of Glory
by — E.W. Bullinger (1837-1913)

There is still something more to learn concerning the Dispensations before we can rightly understand the unique position and wonderful teaching of the later Pauline Epistles written from the prison in Rome.

These Dispensations are commonly spoken of as two, the old and the new, but we must bring them, as all else, to the bar of the written Word to see whether we have learned from man or from God, from tradition or from revelation. To some extent we shall all agree.

### THE FIRST SPHERE OF GLORY:

*Earth*

We shall all be agreed that the great subject of the Old Testament prophecies is a restored Israel and a re-generated earth (Matthew 19:28). It is surely unnecessary to quote the many prophecies which tell of the time when the earth shall be full of the knowledge and glory of the Lord as the waters cover the sea (Numbers 14:21; Psalm 72:19; Isaiah 6:3; 11:9; Habakkuk 2:14).

We are at one with all of our readers in taking these prophecies in their literal meaning; and in not attempting to explain them, or rather fritter them away, by any spiritualizing interpretation which deprives them of all of their truth and power.

We all look forward also to the time when *"He that scattered Israel will gather him"* (Jeremiah 31:10); when they *"shall all be taught of God"* (John 6:45; Isaiah 54:13); when *"the kingdoms of this world shall become the kingdom of our Lord, and of His Christ"* (Revelation 11:15); and when the earthly Jerusalem shall be restored in more than all of its ancient glory.

That kingdom and sphere of blessing and glory will be on the earth, and the new Israel, with a heart of stone changed to a heart of flesh and with a new spirit, will bring forth *"the fruits of righteousness"* (Ezekiel 36:24-36; Matthew 21:43). This will be the regeneration (or *paliggenesia*) when the apostles will be seated *"on twelve thrones judging the twelve tribes of Israel"* (Matthew 19:28). This will be the first and lowest sphere of blessing. It will be on earth, and under the whole heaven. These are the *"people of the saints of the Most High"* (Daniel 7:27). All of the nations of the earth will share in this blessing according to God's original promise to Abraham.[1]

## THE SECOND SPHERE OF GLORY:

### *Heaven*

Abraham and his spiritual seed are *"the saints of the Most High"* as distinct from *"the people"* (of these saints) on the earth (Daniel 7:18, 22, 25), and occupying a distinct place in the heavenly sphere of this same kingdom. These, according to the Lord's words in Luke, are *"equal to the angels," "sons of the resurrection"* (Luke 20:34-36), raised in the *"first resurrection"* before the thousand years of earthly blessing for Israel and for the nations *"under the whole heaven"* (Deuteronomy 4:19; Revelation 20:4-6). These belong to *"that great city, the holy Jerusalem,"* which John saw *"descending down from heaven, having the glory of God; and her light like unto a stone most precious."* This *"holy Jerusalem"* is fully described in Revelation 21:9-27. It is the *"city which hath THE foundations"* for which Abraham had been taught to look (Hebrews 11:10) when he *"saw Christ's day and was glad"* (John

---

1. Genesis 12:3-4; 17:4; Psalm 22:27-28; 67:4; Isaiah 2:4; 11:10, 12; 42:1, 6; 49:22; 52:15; 55:5; 60:3, 5, 11; 66:12, etc.

8:56); for, as *"faith cometh by hearing,"* Abraham must have heard, and this *"hearing"* must have come *" from the* [spoken] *Word of God"* (Romans 10:17).

This is the *"inheritance"* of those who, as Peter declares to the believers of the Dispersion, *"have obtained like precious faith with us."* That *"inheritance"* is *"incorruptible, and undefiled, and fadeth not away, reserved in HEAVEN for you."* The Greek, by the figure *Homoeoteleuton,* emphasizes this *"inheritance"* as being not earthly, but *aphtharton, amianton, amaranton* (I Peter 1:4).

The inhabitants of that heavenly city are declared to be *"the bride, the Lamb's wife"* (Revelation 21:9).

From the call of Abraham there have ever been these two seeds, the earthly and the heavenly. The one was likened by Jehovah to *"the dust of the earth"* or *"the sand of the sea"* (Genesis 13:16; 22:17); and the other was likened to *"the stars of heaven"* (Hebrews 11:12; Genesis 15:5). Both expressions suggest multitude, but the former is especially associated with earthly blessing, while the latter points to *"the partakers of a heavenly calling"* (Hebrews 3:1), who, like their father Abraham, looked for a heavenly portion and a heavenly blessing, for the city *"which hath the foundations."*

> *These all died in faith, not having received the promises, but having seen them and greeted them from afar, and having confessed that they were strangers and pilgrims on the earth. For they that say such things make it manifest that they are seeking after a country of their own. And if indeed they had been mindful of that country from which they came out, they would have had opportunity to return. But now they desire a better country, that is a HEAVENLY; wherefore God is not ashamed of them to be called their God, for He hath prepared for them a city* (Hebrews 11:13-16, *Revised Version*).

Where and what could that city have been if it was not the city which

John was shown *"descending out of heaven from God,"* the foundations of which are specially described in Revelation 21:19-20? Through the ages these were *"partakers of a heavenly calling."* They formed *"the congregation of the Lord,"* and are continually spoken of as such.

Not all of Israel were tabernacle and temple frequenters and worshippers. Not all carried out the laws given by Moses, or offered the prescribed sacrifices, attended *"the feasts of Jehovah,"* or carried out the ordered ritual. Those who gathered to the stated worship of Jehovah are called the *"assembly"* or the *"congregation."*

The Hebrew word for *"congregation"* is from *kāhal* (from which doubtless we have our English word "call"). The verb means *to call, assemble, gather together; and the noun is used of any assembly thus called.* Seventy times in the *Septuagint* version of the Old Testament it is rendered *ekklēsia* (the word for "*church*" in the New Testament).[2]

It is actually used in the expression *"the ekklēsia* [or church] *of the Lord"* in Deuteronomy 23:1-2, 3, 8; I Chronicles 28:8; Micah 2:5. In Nehemiah 13:1 it is *"the ekklēsia* [or church] *of God."* It is this *ekklēsia* (or church) that is referred to as *"the congregation"* in Psalm 22:22; 26:12; 35:18; 40:9-10; 68:26.[3] In Psalm 22:25 it is spoken of as *"the great ekklēsia or congregation,"* and in Psalm 149:1 as *"the ekklēsia of the saints."* This is what David means in Psalm 22 when he says, *"In the midst of the congregation will I praise Thee"* (:22), and *"My praise shall be of Thee in the great congregation"* (:25).

This is the usage of the same word in the Gospels when the Lord said, *"Upon this rock will I build My ekklēsia"* (Matthew 16:18). He did not, when addressing Israelites, use the word in the new, exclusive and special sense in which it was afterward to be used in the revelation of *"the secret"* in the Prison Epistles, but in the larger and wider Old Testament sense which His hearers would understand as embracing

---

2. The Hebrew word is rendered *"congregation"* eighty-six times; *"assembly,"* seventeen times; *"company,"* seventeen times; *"multitude,"* three times.
3. In Numbers 16:3 and 20:4, the Hebrew *kāhal* is rendered in the *Septuagint sunagōgē* = synagogue. In the *R.V.* this is rendered *"the assembly of the Lord."*

## Chapter 2 – Three Spheres of Glory

the whole assembly of Jehovah's believing and worshipping people who were *"partakers of a heavenly calling"* (Hebrews 3:1).

When the Spirit by Stephen speaks of *"the ekklēsia in the wilderness"* (Acts 7:38), He means this congregation of devout worshippers – those who were kept secure *"under the shadow of the Almighty"* during the thirty-eight years of penal wanderings in the wilderness (see Psalm 90-91).

When the Lord added to the *ekklēsia* such as were being saved (Acts 2:47) after Pentecost, He added them to the hundred and twenty who before Pentecost assembled together in the upper room, and who continued daily in the temple [no longer offering sacrifices and partaking of the food furnished thereby], but breaking bread [or eating, as in Luke 24:30, 35 and Acts 27:35] at home, with gladness and singleness of heart, praising God, and having favor with all the people.

*And the Lord added to the church [ekklēsia] daily such as were being saved* (Acts 2:46-47).

When Paul says he *"persecuted the ekklēsia of God"* (I Corinthians 15:9; Galatians 1:13), he does not use the word in a sense of which he had at that time never heard, or had even the remotest idea. His words must be understood in the same sense in which he then used them; and we must not read into any passage of Scripture that which was the subject of a subsequent revelation, especially when the sense is perfectly plain and clear as it stands.

The word *ekklēsia* in the Gospels, Acts and the earlier Pauline Epistles must be taken by us in the sense of its Old Testament (*Septuagint*) usage as meaning simply the congregation, or assembly, or company of Jehovah's worshipping people, *"partakers of a heavenly calling,"* having a heavenly hope, a heavenly sphere of blessing, and looking for their part in the *"resurrection unto life."*

It had been revealed of old that there would be a resurrection (see Job 19:25-27; Hosea 13:14; John 11:24); but it was subsequently revealed also that there would be two resurrections: one to life, and one to judgment. Paul testified of the former as being the hope of those who were worshippers of God (Acts 24:14-15); David hoped for it (Psalm 16:9-11;[4] 49:14-15); so did Daniel (Daniel 12:1-3).

The Lord plainly spoke of the former as *"the resurrection of the just"* (Luke 14:14), and as *"the resurrection of life"* (John 5:29). *"By the Word of the Lord"* was revealed a further hope, or rather, an expression of the hope, in John 11:25-26. There was not only the hope for those who should have part in the *"first resurrection,"* but for those who should be *"alive and remain"* when that event should take place. The *"Word of the Lord"* first mentioned it, and the Holy Spirit by Paul expands it in I Thessalonians 4:16-17.

It concerns the Lord, not only as to His being *"the Resurrection,"* but as to His being *"the Life"* also. He says,

> c | I am the resurrection
> d | and the life.
> c | He that believeth in Me, though he die, he shall live [again]. [To him] I will be *"the resurrection"*
> d | and everyone who [is] alive, and believing in Me shall in nowise die, for the ages. [To him] I will be *"the life"* (John 11:25-26).

This was the hope for all who are *"partakers of a heavenly calling"* (Hebrews 3:1). Many of these were to be found when Messiah came. They were those who:

*waited for the consolation of Israel* (Luke 2:25);

*looked for redemption in Jerusalem* (Luke 2:38);

---

**4.** Though the Psalm refers to Messiah (Acts 2:27-31; 13:35), we may not exclude David himself, though his expectation is *"not yet"* (see Psalm 49:15).

*trusted that the Lord was He Who should have redeemed Israel* (Luke 24:21);

*waited for the kingdom of God* (Mark 15:43; Luke 23:51);

[were] *as many as received Him* (John 1:12);

*gladly received Peter's or Paul's word* [on the Day of Pentecost and after] (Acts 2:41; 8:14; 11:1; 17:11);

*received the Word in much affliction* (I Thessalonians 1:6);

*when they received the Word, accepted it not as man's word, but even as it is truly, God's Word which worketh effectually in you that believe* (I Thessalonians 2:13);

*received not what was promised* [but who believed and embraced it by faith] (Hebrews 11:39).

Which of us has not been in difficulties as to those we speak of as "the Old Testament saints"? Well, here they are seen all through the Old Testament as being "the church [or assembly] of God," "partakers of a heavenly calling," possessing a heavenly hope, and looking for a heavenly sphere of blessing.

## THE THIRD SPHERE OF GLORY:

### *The Highest Heavens*

This brings us to another sphere of blessing, the highest in glory. It had been kept secret *"from ages and from generations."* It is the eonian *"purpose"* of God, made *"before the disruption of the world."* It was a secret not relating to Israel on the earth, nor to the *"partakers of a heavenly calling,"* but to Christ and the elect members of His Body.

The Prison Epistles, following immediately after the proclamation of

Israel's judicial blindness and hardening (recorded in Acts 28:25-26), have for their one great subject the revelation of the final sphere of blessing and glory which stands in special relation to *Christ and His Body*.

- This sphere is not on the earth;
- It is not over the earth;
- It is in the highest heavens.

Hence it has nothing to do with earthly *"signs and wonders"* that would follow those who in happy obedience believe what is there written. Such surpassingly exalted language has never before or since been spoken of human believers. The very glory of that sphere is inconsistent with any earthly signs or manifestations however wonderful, or ordinances however once significant.[5]

The Prison Epistles view the believer of them not with *"signs following,"* but they view him as *"dead"* to this world and all earthly associations and connections, and as having jointly suffered, jointly died, jointly risen and being jointly seated with Christ in the highest heavens. Even the *"affections"* and *"thoughts"* are not to be concerned with the things on earth; they are to be centered on *"the things above,"* where Christ is already seated at the right hand of God.

Hence we do not read in the Prison Epistles about the coming of Christ to the earth, but rather about our being removed to be with Him where He is; not about His *parousia*, or presence on earth, or *"in the air,"* but about our presence and manifestation with Him in His Own glory; not about *anastasis* (or "resurrection," which is the subject of the earlier Pauline Epistles), but about an *exanastasis* (*i.e.*, the out-resurrection, Philippians 3:11), and *"the calling on high"* (:14[6]) which is the subject of the later Epistles; not about any personal happiness which we may have, but about Christ's personal

---

5. It may even be that they are appropriate for the *"partakers of a heavenly calling,"* although they may be unthinkable by those who realize their position as described in Colossians 1:12-14; 2:20.
6. It is quite incorrect to render the Greek *anō* as *"high,"* as though it was an adjective qualifying the character of that *"calling,"* because it is an adverb, denoting its direction.

glory, in which we have the wondrous privilege of sharing.

In this connection we would call attention to one word which, in our judgment, is the real key-word of the Prison Epistles, and of the highest sphere. It is a remarkable word, found in this form, only here in the New Testament. It occurs once before in Romans 13:9, but there it is in the Present Passive voice (*anakephalaioutai*), and means "is summed up." However in Ephesians 1:10 it is the Aorist Infinitive of the Middle voice (*anakephalaiosasthai*). This difference is ignored both by the *Authorized* and the *Revised Versions*, which read the Middle voice of Ephesians 1:10 as though it were the Active. This is an almost unpardonable oversight, in the interest of the ordinary Bible reader, who has an undoubted right to a correct grammatical rendering from such a quarter.

Translated correctly, the word and the entire passage emphasize the underlying fact that in all things there revealed, our Heavenly Father has, *for Himself,* purposed what is here stated, *viz.,* that,

> *according to His good pleasure, which He purposed in Himself, in order to a dispensation of the fullness of the seasons, TO-SUM-UP-FOR-HIMSELF, everything in Christ: things in heaven and things on earth, even in Him, in Whom we were taken as an inheritance, being foreordained according to the purpose of Him Who worketh all things according to the council of His Own will, that we should be to the praise of His glory who have before hoped in Christ.*

This will be enough to show us that the *kosmos*, as shown in Colossians 1:15-16, is a larger, higher and greater degree than that of earthly glory, or that of the glory reserved for those who are *"partakers of a heavenly calling."*

The Old Testament, the Acts and the earlier Pauline Epistles deal with the *lower* sphere of glory, but the later Epistles reveal a sphere of headship and heirship *above* the earth or the heavens. I Corinthians 15:40

tells of *"terrestrial"* glory and of *"celestial"* glory, which differ the one from the other; but there is a sphere of *cosmical* glory (if we may use the word in this connection) *high above all* created beings, whether principalities, or powers, or might, or thrones, or dominions, which are mentioned (though not defined or explained) in Ephesians 1:21; Colossians 1:16 in relation to Christ, Who shall be *"Head over all."*

# Chapter 3

## The Three Spheres

by — Charles H. Welch (1880-1967)

## The Earth – The New Jerusalem – Far Above All

There are three spheres of blessing: the Earth, the heavenly city, and the position indicated in Ephesians 1, as *"far above all."*

This aspect of truth is vital. It gathers up unto itself all that is distinctive in what is called "Dispensational Truth," and we must spare no pains, nor begrudge the space needed to provide the scriptural evidence for believing these three spheres of blessing revealed in the Scriptures.

We will enumerate in scriptural terms the actual spheres of blessing spoken of in the Scriptures, and then compare and contrast them so that by trying the things that differ we may avoid confusion and keep each calling in its appointed place.

### "IN HEAVENLY PLACES"

Let us begin with our own calling as revealed in the Epistle to the Ephesians.

*Blessed be the God and Father of our Lord Jesus Christ, Who hath blessed us with all spiritual blessings* **in heavenly places** *in Christ* (1:3).

At the moment we are not concerned with the kind of blessings here set forth, namely, *"spiritual,"* but with the *province, range* or *domain* in which these blessings naturally find their setting. The sphere of blessing found here is defined as *"in heavenly places."*

Again, we are not *yet* concerned as to whether these *"heavenly places"* are no higher than the firmament in which birds fly; whether they denote the starry heavens; or whether they refer to a position far above all. All that we are immediately concerned with is that a distinct sphere is indicated by the words ***"in heavenly places."***

## *"The Earth"*

We now turn to another part of the New Testament, where we read of another sphere of blessing:

> *Blessed are the meek, for they shall inherit* **the earth** (Matthew 5:5).

A sphere of blessing is found in Matthew 5:5 which is defined as *"the earth."* Once more, we are not concerned with the character of those here referenced, nor with their inheritance, but exclusively with the *sphere* of their inheritance.

We assume, but have not yet proved, that *"the earth"* and *"heavenly places"* are two distinct spheres. Common sense says they are distinct, but we leave the proof until later.

Here then are two spheres of blessing concerning which there is no controversy, but in addition to these two we discover what appears to be an intermediate sphere of blessing, a sphere above *"the earth,"* yet not *"in heavenly places."* For this we turn to Galatians 3:14.

> *That the blessing of Abraham might come on the Gentiles through Jesus Christ.*

## Chapter 3 – The Three Spheres

The question which now arises is, does this passage refer to a distinct sphere of blessing, or is the blessing of Abraham to be enjoyed in one or other of the two spheres already considered? A complete answer can be given only after careful examination, but for the sake of conciseness, we note that in this calling,

> *there is neither Jew nor Greek, there is neither bond nor free, there is neither male nor female, for ye are all one in Christ Jesus* (Galatians 3:28).

This unity does not sound like the constitution of a kingdom, which is what is in view in Matthew 5. Rather it so resembles the later revelation of Ephesians that some have adopted the expression *"all one in Christ Jesus"* with the idea that it declares the Unity of the spirit of Ephesians 4.

Before seeing the proofs, most, if not all, will agree that Galatians 3:14 does not refer to an inheritance on *"the earth."* Yet when we read on to Galatians 3:29, we are prevented from asserting that it belongs to the sphere of the Mystery made known in Ephesians, for we find it stated,

> *And if ye be Christ's, then are ye Abraham's seed, and heirs according to the promise.*

So entirely contrary is it to the scriptural teaching concerning the Mystery to make it a fulfillment of any promise to Abraham that we must hesitate to place this company, which is Abraham's seed, *"in heavenly places."*

We therefore search further in this epistle, and in the chapter 4 we find the following statement:

> *But Jerusalem which is above is free, which is the mother of us all ... now we, brethren, as Isaac was, are the children of promise* (4:26, 28).

## "THE HEAVENLY JERUSALEM"

*"Jerusalem which is above,"* is neither *"on the earth"* nor *"in heavenly places far above all principality,"* and as this city forms the theme of Hebrews 11:9-16 and 12:18-23, where it is contrasted with the *"earth,"* we are obliged to record a third sphere of blessing.

A third sphere of blessing, differing from that of Ephesians 1:3 and that of Matthew 5:5, is recorded in the Epistles to the Galatians and the Hebrews, and is associated with *"the heavenly Jerusalem"* (Hebrews 12:22), a sphere distinct on the one hand from Earth and its kingdom, and on the other hand from the heavenly places which are the sphere of the church[1] of the Mystery.

We therefore set out our first conclusion.

### The Three Spheres of Blessings

| "The Earth" | Matthew 5:5 | The Kingdom |
| --- | --- | --- |
| "Jerusalem which is above" | Galatians 4:26 | The Bride |
| "In heavenly places" | Ephesians 1:3 | The Body |

In the near context of Matthew 5:5, which speaks of the meek who shall *"inherit the earth,"* we learn of a kingdom which is yet to be set up on Earth:

*Thy Kingdom come. Thy will be done in Earth, as it is in Heaven* (Matthew 6:10).

In that prophecy of His Second Coming, The Revelation, one of the titles of the Lord is: *"The Prince of the Kings of the Earth"* (Revelation 1:5). The extent of this kingdom is defined in Psalm 72:8.

---

1. [*Editor:*] The Greek word often translated as *"church"* in most English versions is ἐκκλησία (*ekklēsia,* or ecclesia). The word is a compound word meaning "called-out" (*ek* = "out"; *kaleō* = called). The ecclesia is God's "called-out" ones. The ecclesia is not a building or denomination; not a meeting, or doctrinal creed; it is not somewhere we go, or something we do, it is who we as believers *are*.

## Chapter 3 – The Three Spheres

> *He shall have dominion also from sea to sea, and from the river unto the ends of the earth.*

Again, in Psalm 2:8.

> *Ask of Me, and I shall give Thee the heathen, Thine inheritance, and the uttermost parts of the earth, Thy possession.*

Yet again, the prophet Zechariah says:

> *He shall speak peace unto the heathen: and His dominion shall be from sea even to sea, and from the river even to the ends of the earth* (9:10).

Moreover, in The Revelation we read:

> *The seventh angel sounded; and there were great voices in Heaven, saying, "The kingdoms of this world are become the kingdoms of our Lord, and of His Christ …"* (11:15).

This kingdom on Earth will have an administrative center:

> *It shall come to pass in the last days, that the mountain of the Lord's house shall be established in the top of the mountains, and shall be exalted above the hills; and all nations shall flow unto it. And many people shall go and say, "Come ye, and let us go up to the mountain of the Lord, to the house of the God of Jacob; and He will teach us of His ways, and we will walk in His paths: for out of Zion shall go forth the law, and the Word of the Lord from Jerusalem"* (Isaiah 2:2-3).

This is supplemented by Zechariah the prophet:

> *It shall come to pass, that every one that is left of all the nations which came against Jerusalem shall even go up from year to year to worship the King, the Lord of hosts, and to keep the feast of*

*Tabernacles. And it shall be that whoso will not come up of all the families of the earth unto Jerusalem to worship the King, the Lord of hosts, even upon them shall be no rain* (14:16-17).

It will be seen by the two latter references from Isaiah and Zechariah that, not only is the city of Jerusalem represented as the capital of the kingdom, but also as the center of worship, and this is in harmony with the destiny of Israel when that nation is at length saved, for Israel is to be a kingdom of priests unto God (Revelation 1:6).

They will be made so under the New Covenant and the blood of Christ in fulfillment of the original purpose of God expressed at the foot of Mount Sinai but, by reason of the weakness of the flesh, rendered impossible of accomplishment under the law (Exodus 19:6).

Inasmuch as the bulk of Scripture is taken up with the history and prophecy of this earthly people and kingdom, no attempt on our part, particularly considering the limitations of our space, can possibly do more than indicate the fact of its existence.

There is, however, unanimity among most believers regarding this first, or lowest sphere of blessing, and while we shall have to return to the subject when certain of its features will be compared with those of other spheres, we now pass on to the consideration of the next sphere, having left nothing unproved or resting upon mere assumption.

Earth will be a sphere of blessing in which there shall be set up a kingdom, over which the Lord shall be King, with Jerusalem the chosen center, and Israel a Kingdom of Priests. This we will call the First Sphere.

We now come to the second sphere; that which is associated with the heavenly Jerusalem, and it must be recorded as a fact of importance that no hint of such a sphere is to be found in the whole of the Old Testament. Yet when we study the New Testament we learn that its existence was intimately known by Abraham, Isaac and Jacob. For

## Chapter 3 – The Three Spheres

this information we turn to the Epistle to the Hebrews.

In Hebrews 11 the apostle illustrates the statement that *"faith is the substance of things hoped for, the evidence of things not seen,"* by the examples of Abel, Enoch, Noah, Abraham, Isaac and Jacob. Coming to the example of the patriarchs, the writer pauses to add,

> *By faith he [Abraham] sojourned in the land of promise, as in a strange country, dwelling in tabernacles [tents] with Isaac and Jacob, the heirs with him of the same promise: for he looked for a city which hath foundations, whose Builder and Maker is God* (11:9-10).

After speaking of Sarah's faith, the apostle reverts to the subject of this city, saying,

> *These all died in faith, not having received the promises, but having seen them afar off, and were persuaded of them, and embraced them, and confessed that they were strangers and pilgrims on the earth. For they that say such things declare plainly that they seek a country ... that is, a heavenly: wherefore God is not ashamed to be called their God; for He hath prepared for them a city* (:13-16).

After a further and fuller expansion of the theme of Hebrews 11:1 the apostle returns to the subject of the Heavenly City in chapter 12, but approaches it from another angle. We reserve comment upon the significance of this new angle until we have established the fact of the revelation of all three spheres, and meantime pass on to :22-23:

> *But ye are come unto Mount Zion, and unto the city of the living God, the heavenly Jerusalem, and to an innumerable company of angels, to the general assembly and church of the firstborn, which are written in heaven.*

Other references to this sphere of blessing are found in The Revelation:

> *Him that overcometh will I make a pillar in the temple of My God, and he shall go no more out: and I will write upon him the name of My God, and the name of the city of My God, which is new Jerusalem, which cometh down out of Heaven from my God: and I will write upon him My new name* (3:12).

The significance of the fact that this is associated with the overcomer, together with the similar significance of the context of Hebrews 12, will be considered when we come to deal with the subject of the spheres themselves: at present we confine ourselves to establishing the fact that the Scriptures speak of such spheres:

> *And I John saw the holy city, new Jerusalem, coming down from God out of heaven, prepared as a bride adorned for her husband* (Revelation 21:2).

> *He carried me away in the spirit to a great and high mountain, and showed me that great city, the holy Jerusalem, descending out of Heaven from God* (:10).

The testimony of Hebrews 11:16 alone is sufficient proof that this *heavenly city* is a separate sphere of blessing from that of the Earth, and while much must yet be studied if we would appreciate its true significance, we can, without hesitation, affirm that there is full Scriptural testimony to the existence of this second sphere of blessing.

Granting that these two spheres of blessing are actual Scriptural facts, the question that now awaits an answer is: Do they exhaust the teaching of Scripture on the subject?

In other words, is there a third sphere of blessing distinct from both the Earth and the *heavenly city*? We believe there is, and proceed at once to state the evidence for this belief.

The epistle to the Ephesians was written by Paul as *"the prisoner of Jesus Christ"* (Ephesians 3:1). Israel, as a nation, had been set aside by

## Chapter 3 – The Three Spheres

the quoting of Isaiah 6:10, as recorded in Acts 28, and with that setting aside had of necessity gone the hope and the blessings of which they were the appointed channel.

While Israel remained as a nation before God, the Gentile believer could be *"blessed with faithful Abraham"* (Galatians 3:9); could be associated with Israel under the *"New Covenant"* (II Corinthians 3:6); could entertain the hope of Israel (Romans 15:12-13); and could *"partake of the root and fatness of the olive tree"* (Romans 11:17).

However, with Israel set aside, there arose the necessity of a further revelation from God, if all was not to be plunged into confusion and end in despair. This revelation is claimed by Paul in the epistle to the Ephesians:

> *If ye have heard of the **dispensation** of the grace of God which is given me to you-ward* [Gentiles]: *how that by **revelation** He made known unto me the Mystery* (3:2-3).

This Mystery has particular reference to the new position assigned to the Gentiles:

> *That the Gentiles should be fellowheirs, and of the same body, and partakers of His promise in Christ by the gospel: whereof I was made a minister* (3:6-7).

Here we have a *"dispensation"* which was particularly concerned with the Gentiles; a *"revelation"* that makes known that which was a *"mystery,"* and that, hitherto, this mystery had been *"hid in God"* (:9).

Not only was it *"hid in God,"* but *"from the ages and from generations,"* but NOW is *"made manifest to His saints"* (Colossians 1:26).

In order that no statement shall be accepted as true that is not proved from the Scriptures, we pause to justify the remark that *the dispensation of the Mystery was revealed after the setting aside of Israel.*

Usually it is enough to produce the missing link in a chain; but, if the play of words may be pardoned, we have a complete chain of evidence, and that none other than the one which fettered the apostle Paul in his Roman prison.

Until the conference with the leaders of the Jews which concluded with their dismissal at the quoting of Isaiah 6, there was the human possibility of the national repentance of Israel and the realization of that nation's hope. Consequently, the apostle rightly says in Acts 28:20,

> *For the hope of Israel I am bound with this chain.*

The next time he speaks of his bonds as his chain, the *Dispensation of the Mystery* had been entrusted to him, and in Ephesians and Colossians his chain is most intimately associated with *the Mystery* (Ephesians 6:20; Colossians 4:3).

While there is much more to be said concerning the unique character of this *new revelation*, enough has been adduced to prove beyond dispute that this *Dispensation of the Mystery*, revealed after the setting aside of Israel, must be different from both the earthly sphere and the new Jerusalem, and as we have seen that these latter terms represent two very distinct spheres, we are compelled to subscribe to the doctrine of three spheres of blessing, thus:

1. **First Sphere: The Earth**

    – *Subject of Old Testament and part of New Testament.*
    – Israel dominant.

2. **Second Sphere: New Jerusalem**

    – *Subject only of part of the New Testament.*
    – Both Jew and Gentile as seed of Abraham.

# Chapter 3 – The Three Spheres

## 3. Third Sphere: The Mystery

- *Subject of the Prison Epistles only.*
- *Gentiles especially.*

We have considered, a little more in detail, the characteristics of that sphere of blessing which belongs to Israel and the earth. We must now turn our attention to the next sphere, the one associated with the heavenly Jerusalem. The two epistles that speak of the heavenly Jerusalem are Galatians and Hebrews, and we must now acquaint ourselves with their teaching.

Dr. J.W. Thirtle, in two articles (from which we quote),[2] presented a good case for his contention that the epistle to the Galatians was a *cover letter*, and that the epistle to the Hebrews was an *enclosure* written, in the first case, for the Hebrews in the Churches of Galatia.

> What in reality do we find? Just this – two epistles, or writings, in close succession, in a professedly Pauline section of the New Testament, are merely separated or divided off, the one from the other, by the words *pros Hebraious* "to Hebrews."
>
> Both epistles quote Habakkuk 2:4, *"The just shall live by faith"* (Galatians 3:11; Hebrews 10:38), both develop the allegory of Sinai and Zion (Galatians 4:24-31; Hebrews 12:18-24), both deal with *"perfection"* (Galatians 3:3, Hebrews throughout), both speak of Jerusalem which is above, and both speak of the Mediator.

Another very cogent argument which supports this connection is the fact that, although circumcision is at the very heart of the Jewish problem, the apostle never speaks of it in the epistle to the Hebrews. This would be difficult to explain or to understand if Hebrews stood alone, but if Galatians and Hebrews go together, then circumcision would have been effectively dealt with in the *cover letter,* leaving the way clear in Hebrews for the exhortation that it gives to go on to perfection.

---
2. Contributed to *The Christian* of April 27th and May 4th, 1916.

The first definite indication of *the sphere of blessing* that is in view in the epistle to the Hebrews is found in chapter 3:1, where those to whom the apostle wrote are called *"holy brethren, partakers of the heavenly calling."*

This is the first of six occurrences of *epouranios*[3] in Hebrews, which we give below:

> *Wherefore, holy brethren, partakers of the heavenly calling, consider the Apostle and High Priest of our profession, Christ Jesus* (3:1).

> *For it is impossible for those who were once enlightened, and have tasted of the heavenly gift, and were made partakers of the Holy Spirit ... to renew them again unto repentance* (6:4-6).

> *Who serve unto the example and shadow of heavenly things, as Moses was admonished of God when he was about to make the tabernacle: for, "See," saith He, "that thou make all things according to the pattern showed to thee in the mount"* (8:5).

> *It was therefore necessary that the patterns of things in the heavens should be purified with these; but the heavenly things themselves with better sacrifices than these* (9:23).

> *But now they desire a better country, that is, an heavenly: wherefore God is not ashamed to be called their God: for He hath prepared for them a city* (11:16).

> *But ye are come unto mount Zion, and unto the city of the living God, the heavenly Jerusalem* (12:22).

We must now examine these passages, so that our conception of what is "heavenly" shall be molded, not by our own views, but by what is actually written.

---

3. *[Editor:] Strong's* G2032.

## Chapter 3 – The Three Spheres

In the first passage, we read that these Hebrews were *"partakers of the heavenly calling,"* but whether or not this means that they were going to enjoy their inheritance in the heavenly places *"where Christ sitteth"* is not here stated.

In the first place, however, let us note that there is the most positive testimony that the position occupied by Christ in Hebrews is identical with that of Ephesians.

In Ephesians, Christ is said to have ascended *"far above all heavens"* (4:10), while in Hebrews He is said to have *"passed through the heavens"* (4:14) and *"made higher than the heavens"* (hupseloteros,[4] 7:26).

What is never taught in Hebrews, however, is that any of the redeemed could entertain the hope of being there, *"where Christ sitteth."* The teaching is all in the other direction. We are reminded, for instance, that when the High Priest entered the most holy place (a type of Heaven itself) he entered *"alone"* (9:7). These Hebrews had certainly *"tasted the heavenly gift,"* but they did not ascend to Heaven to do so; they tasted this heavenly gift while *here on Earth*.

It is therefore folly to point to the fact that the [Greek] word *epouranios* occurs both in Hebrews and in Ephesians, and to deduce from this that there is nothing distinctive about the Ephesian sphere.

In Hebrews it is Christ, and Christ *"alone,"* Who sits in the heavenly place. In Ephesians, the essence of *the Mystery* is that an elect company of the redeemed sit there with Him. It is this fact that makes this *new sphere* of blessing unique; a fact which an indiscriminate list of the occurrences of *epouranios* can neither establish nor overthrow.

While Hebrews speaks of a *"heavenly calling"* and a *"heavenly gift,"* we are not left in doubt as to *where* this calling is to be enjoyed. The sphere of blessing connected with the *"heavenly calling"* is the *"heavenly Jerusalem"* which filled the vision of Abraham, and for which

---

**4.** [*Editor:*] Both *Young's* and *Strong's* (G5308) have *hupselos*, i.e., "higher."

those who walked by faith in the Old Testament days suffered the loss of all things.

> *Now faith is the substance of things hoped for, the evidence of things not seen ... these all died in faith, not having received the promises, but having seen them afar off, and were persuaded of them, and embraced them, and confessed that they were strangers and pilgrims on the earth . . . wherefore God ... hath prepared for them a city* (11:1, 13, 16).

This calling differs from the one that is associated with Mount Sinai. Abraham, Isaac and Jacob were all *"before the law"* (see Galatians 3:17-18), and the inclusion of Abel, Noah and Enoch shows that it is not essentially connected with the Abrahamic covenant.

Moreover the inclusion of Rahab, after the law, reveals that it is of wider scope than the covenant of Sinai, and the presence of such names as Gideon, Barak, Samson, Jephthah, David and Samuel (Hebrews 11:32) shows that after the law of Moses had been given, there were still those who reached out for this higher and heavenly sphere.

In contrast with Sinai and its terrors, we have Zion with its blessings.

> *Ye are come unto mount Sion, and unto the city of the living God, the heavenly Jerusalem, and to an innumerable company of angels, to the general assembly, and to a church of firstborn ones, which are written in heaven, and to God the Judge of all, and to the spirits of perfected righteous ones, and to Jesus the Mediator of the new covenant, and to the blood of sprinkling, that speaketh better things than Abel* (12:22-24).

The reader will notice a slight departure from the *A.V.* here. The *"general assembly"* should be linked, not with the *"church of the firstborn,"* but with the *"innumerable company."* The church of the firstborn is made up of *"the spirits of perfected righteous ones"* (:23), or *"the spirits of righteous ones having been perfected."* This *"perfecting"* is the key to

Hebrews and is the basis of its exhortation.

Either those to whom the Apostle wrote would leave the things that were connected with the beginning and go on unto perfection (6:1), or, failing to endure, would draw back unto *"loss"* and *"waste"* (10:32-39).

It is clear from Hebrews 11 and 12 that the sphere of blessing there in view is that of the city which will at the last come down from God *out of Heaven*. This reference takes us to the Book of the Revelation, where we discover two things.

First, that those whose blessings are found in the New Jerusalem are spoken of as the *"Bride,"* a company that differs from the divorced *"Wife"* who will be restored at the end; and secondly, that this company are *"overcomers"* who have a *"crown"* (3:11-12).

We discover, therefore, that the second sphere of blessing is in the nature of a reward. It is the "*heavenly*" phase of the *earthly* kingdom. Abraham could not have forfeited the land of promise, for it was his as an unconditional gift; but in addition to this, he received the *"heavenly,"* which was associated with his *"perfecting."*

This *"perfecting"* of his faith is the theme of the Epistle of James, which regards the offering of Isaac as the *"fulfilling"* of the initial act of faith whereby Abraham was justified (2:23).

James also has much to say in the first chapter about patient endurance and its perfecting work in view of the crown (1:3-4, 12). The *heavenly city* is not for righteous ones, simply, but for *perfected* righteous ones.

If the *heavenly country* for which Abraham gave up so much differs from the land of promise in which he lived as a pilgrim, then we must obviously recognize this *"heavenly calling"* as a separate sphere. Moreover it is clear that one of the chief characteristics of this sphere is that it represents a reward for faithful obedience, as distinct from the land of promise which was quite unconditional.

We have not attempted to differentiate between the covenant made with Abraham regarding the land, and the covenant made at Sinai. As both operate *on the earth,* they are both included in the one sphere.

The distinctive place *where* and the time *when* the Church of the Mystery shall enjoy its blessings, and was chosen in Christ by the Father, are given in Ephesians 1:3-4. We are not now concerned with the true translation of the words, *"before the foundation of the world"* (:4), but with the latter clause of :3.

> *Blessed be the God and Father of our Lord Jesus Christ, Who hath blessed us with all spiritual blessings **in heavenly places** in Christ.*

"In heavenly places" is the translation of the Greek words *en tois epouraniois*. *Epouranios* occurs six times in the Epistle to the Hebrews, but there it speaks of a *"heavenly calling,"* a *"heavenly gift,"* *"heavenly"* realities, and a *"heavenly"* city.

There can be no comparison between a *"heavenly gift"* that was enjoyed *on Earth* with *"the heavenly places"* of Ephesians 1:3. The one refers to character, the other to a place.

The occurrences of *epouranios* in Ephesians must be segregated, for they form a group by themselves. The phrase *en tois epouraniois* occurs only in Ephesians and nowhere else.

The second occurrence of the phrase is found in Ephesians 1:20-21, where we learn that this sphere is *"where Christ sitteth"* at the right hand of God. Nothing is more certain than that there can be no conceivably higher position in the whole universe than the right hand of God. Such is the height of this exaltation of Christ that the passage continues:

***Far above all*** *principality, and power, and might, and dominion, and every name that is named, not only in this world, but also in that which is to come* (:21).

Quite apart from the words *"far above all,"* there can be no denial of the fact that there is here indicated a sphere without comparison in the whole range of Scripture. To conclude the first part of our examination, we turn to Ephesians 2:6 where we have a categorical statement that there, where Christ sits, is the sphere of blessing for every member of the Church which is His Body.

In these three passages (1:3; 1:20-21; 2:6) we have indubitable evidence of a sphere of blessing that differs entirely from anything that had hitherto been revealed.

Of no other company of believers is it said that their sphere of blessing is *"in the super-heavenlies."* The special sphere of blessing which belongs alone to the Church of the One Body is mentioned five times in this epistle, and a study of these occurrences will supply us with valuable information.

First of all, we translate the word *"super-heavenlies"* in recognition of the presence of the little particle *epi* with which the word begins. It is not simply *ouranos*,[5] which is the usual word, but *epouranios*.

Secondly, the information supplied by the five references demands some such translation. Passing, therefore, to the second reference, we find, in 1:20-21, that this sphere of blessing is,

(a) At the Father's right hand.
(b) Far above all principality and power.

That this tremendous height is the destined sphere of the Church of the Mystery, 2:6 declares. There the believer is associated with the risen Christ,

---
5. [*Editor:*] Strong's G3772.

*... made to sit together in the super-heavenlies in Christ Jesus.*

Christ the Head and the Church His Body are blessed together *there*.

The next two references (3:10; 6:12), show the super-heavenlies as the abode of principalities, powers and rulers. Be it noted that angels are not mentioned. Angels are heaven's messengers. The Church of the One Body is blessed even above heaven's nobility. Dominions and thrones are beneath it in its super-heavenly sphere ... While *epouranios* is used outside Ephesians, no other company of believers is blessed *IN* these exalted regions as their sphere. The blessings of the Church of the One Body are not only *"heavenly,"* but *up in Heaven*.

Having established from the Scriptures, quite independently of the occurrences or the meaning of either *epouranios* or *huperano*,[6] the fact that there are three distinct companies of believers who are destined to inherit blessings in three distinct spheres, we can dismiss the question as to how *far* this exalted sphere is above all others; the answer to the question makes no difference to the fact that the Scriptures speak of three different spheres. For the sake of clarity we summarize our findings.

## The *Earthly* Sphere

There are blessings that are to be enjoyed on Earth. Those who will occupy the central position in this sphere are Israel, and this calling is expressed in the terms of a *"Kingdom."*

Gentile nations, while blessed in this same sphere, will be subservient, for to Israel, and Israel alone, is the Kingdom. Israel is the firstborn among the nations.

## The *Heavenly* Sphere

There are other blessings that are to be enjoyed *"in the holy city, new Jerusalem,* **coming down from God out of Heaven"** (Revelation

---

6. [*Editor:*] *Strong's* G5231, "far above."

21:2). These are the blessings of Abraham, and the calling is that of *"the Bride"* (a calling that must be kept distinct from that of the restoration of Israel, *"the Wife"*). Gentiles, as well as Israel, go to form this company called *"the Bride,"* where there is neither Jew nor Greek, but where both alike are reckoned as Abraham's seed and heirs according to the promise.

Instead of nations being subservient to this company of the redeemed, it is angels who are associated with them in a subordinate position. This company in this sphere is the church of the Firstborn whose names are written in heaven.

## THE *SUPER-HEAVENLY* SPHERE

There are, however, blessings that are neither those of Israel as a kingdom, nor of the heavenly calling of the Bride, and these are enjoyed in *"heavenly places"* where Christ sits, *"far above all"* principality and power and *"far above all heavens"* (Ephesians 4:10).

They who enjoy these constitute neither a Kingdom nor the Bride, but are the Body of Christ and a perfect Man. While individuals of Israel who believe today are not precluded, this calling is mainly Gentile, for it operates during the period of Israel's blindness.

This company also has a citizenship, but it is one which has nothing to do with either the earth or the New Jerusalem; not merely nation or angels are subservient to it, but principalities and powers.

To this company pertains the Firstborn from the dead, is its Head, each believer of the company forming a member of the Church which is His Body.

As this highest of all callings is the subject of THE SECRET that goes back before the overthrow of the world (Genesis 1:2), so it *goes up beyond* the *"firmament that was called heaven"* which spans the ages, and finds its sphere in *the super-heavens*; those heavens of Genesis

1:1 which remain unmoved by the ebb and flow of time, sin, death or dispensational change.[7]

---

7. [*Editor:*] For more studies on these three spheres, see:
   – *Three Spheres of Glory*, Dr. E.W. Bullinger, *Bible Student's Notebook* 596;
   – *The Three Spheres: Distinguishing Between Them*, H.W. Fry, *Bible* Student's Notebook #613.

# Chapter 4

## The Hope of the Third Sphere
by — Charles H. Welch (1880-1967)

## Manifestation in Glory

*B*efore considering the special characteristics of the hope of the church[1] of the One Body, it may be of service to set out some of the distinctive features of the *Dispensation of the Mystery*,[2] so that, perceiving the unique character of its calling, we shall be compelled to believe the unique character of its hope.

### SPECIAL FEATURES OF THE PRESENT DISPENSATION

First of all, let us observe two features that marked the previous dispensation but are now absent.

**Presence and Prominence of Israel**

The testimony of the Gospels (Matthew 10:6; 15:24), the witness of Peter (Acts 3:25-26), and the testimony of Paul (Romans 1:16; 3:29; 9:1-5; 11:24-25; 15:8), all combine to show that the nation of Israel was an

---

1. [*Editor:*] The Greek word often translated as "*church*" in most English versions is ἐκκλησία (*ekklēsia,* or ecclesia). The word is a compound word meaning "called-out" (*ek* = "out"; *kaleō* = called). The ecclesia is God's "called-out" ones. The ecclesia is not a building or denomination; not a meeting, or doctrinal creed; it is not somewhere we go, or something we do, it is who we as believers *are*.
2. [*Editor:*] or, the *Administration of the Secret*. For more information on this theme see:
   – *The Present Secret Administration*, A.E. Knoch, <u>Bible Student's Notebook #575</u>;
   – *A New Administration at the Close of Acts*, Adlai Loudy, *Part 1* – <u>Bible Student's Notebook #562</u>; *Part 2* – <u>Bible Student's Notebook # 563</u>;
   – *The Pentecost, Readjustment & Secret Administrations*, Adlai Loudy, <u>Bible Student's Notebook #497</u>.

important factor in the outworking of the purpose of the ages, and that, during the period covered by the Gospels and the Acts, no blessing could be enjoyed by a Gentile independent of Israel. It is evident that with the setting aside of this favored people, a change in dispensation was necessitated.

### Presence and Prominence of Miraculous Gifts

Throughout the public ministry of the Lord Jesus, and from Pentecost in Acts 2 until the shipwreck on the island of Melita in Acts 28, supernatural signs, wonders and miracles accompanied and confirmed the preached word. Not only did the Lord Himself and also His apostles work miracles, but during the time of the Acts ordinary members of the church were in possession of spiritual gifts in such abundance that they had to seek the Apostle's advice as to their regulation in the assembly (I Corinthians 14:26-40). The miracles of Mark 16, Acts 2 and I Corinthians 12-14 are not the normal experience of the church of today. Their absence, together with the setting aside of the people of Israel, constitute two pieces of negative evidence in favor of a new dispensation. We are not, however, limited to negative evidence. Scripture also provides definite evidence of a positive kind, which we must now consider.

## THE DISPENSATIONAL BOUNDARY OF ACTS 28

Right up to the last chapter of the Acts, Israel and miraculous gifts continued to occupy their pre-eminent place (Acts 28:1-10, 17, 20). Upon arrival at Rome, Paul, although desirous of visiting the saints (*cf.* Romans 1:11-13), sent first for the *"chief* [among] *the Jews,"* telling them that *"for the hope of Israel"* he was bound with a chain. After spending a whole day with these men of Israel, seeking unsuccessfully to persuade them *"concerning Jesus"* out of the law and the prophets, he pronounces finally their present doom of blindness, adding:

> Be it known therefore unto you, that the salvation of God is sent unto the Gentiles, and that they will hear it (Acts 28:28).

During the two years of imprisonment that followed, the Apostle ministered to all who came to him, teaching those things which *"concern the Lord Jesus Christ"* with no reference this time either to the law or to the prophets (:30-31).

## THE PRESENT DISPENSATION A NEW REVELATION

The omission of *"the law and the prophets"* from Acts 28:31, as compared with :23, is an important point. Throughout the early ministry of the Apostle he makes continual and repeated appeal to the Old Testament Scriptures. However, when one examines the Prison Epistles one is struck by the absence of quotation. The reason for this change is that Paul, as the prisoner of Jesus Christ for the Gentiles, received the Mystery *"by revelation"* (Ephesians 3:1-3). This Mystery had been hidden from ages and generations, until the time came for Paul to be made its minister (Colossians 1:24-27). It could not, therefore, be found in the Old Testament Scriptures.

## SOME SPECIAL FEATURES OF THIS NEW CALLING

- This church was chosen *"before the foundation of the world"* (Ephesians 1:4) and *"before age-times"* (II Timothy 1:9).

- This church finds its sphere of blessing, ...

   *in heavenly places, far above all principality and power ... seated together in heavenly places in Christ Jesus* (Ephesians 1:3, 20-21; 2:6).

- This church is not an *evolution*, but a *new creation*, the peculiar advantage of being a Jew, even though a member of the church, having disappeared with the middle wall of partition (Ephesians 2:14-19).

- This church is the One Body of which Christ is the Head, and in which all members are equal (Ephesians 1:22-23; 3:6), a relationship never before known.

## The Prison Epistles

While the very nature of things demands a new dispensation consequent upon Israel's removal, we are not left to mere inference. One definite section of the New Testament includes special teaching relating to the church of the present dispensation. This is found in the epistles written by Paul as the prisoner of the Lord for us Gentiles. These epistles are generally referred to as the Prison Epistles.[3]

The Prison Epistles are:

A. EPHESIANS

> The Dispensation of the Mystery
> *Basic Truth*

   B. PHILIPPIANS

> Prize
> *Outworking*

A. COLOSSIANS

> The Dispensation of the Mystery
> *Basic Truth*

   B. II TIMOTHY

> The Crown
> *Outworking*

The reader will find, in each of these epistles, evidence that they were written from prison and that they form part of the ministry referred to in Acts 28:31.

---

3. Philemon is practical and personal and makes no contribution to the new teaching.

# Chapter 4 – The Hope of the Third Sphere

## THE NEW SPHERE OF HOPE NECESSITATES PRAYER

While prayer should accompany the Word at all times, there is no need to pray for "revelation" concerning one's hope if it be already revealed. Words can scarcely be clearer than those employed in I Thessalonians 4, and, if this chapter still represented the hope of the church of the One Body, there would be no need for the Apostle to speak as he does in Ephesians 1:17-18, where he prays that the saints might receive,

> *the spirit of wisdom and revelation in the knowledge of Him ... that ye may know what is the hope of His calling.*

## THE NEW SPHERE OF HOPE ASSOCIATED WITH A PROMISE

Hope and promise are necessarily linked together. The promises that were the basis of expectation during the Acts were the promises *"made unto the fathers."* Now, the fathers had no promises made to them concerning heavenly places *"where Christ sitteth at the right hand of God."* They knew nothing of a church where Gentile believers would be on perfect equality with Jewish believers. The promises made to the fathers never extended beyond *"the Bride"* or *"the Heavenly Jerusalem,"* but in Ephesians we have *"the Body"* and a sphere *"far above all."*

In Ephesians 1:12, where the A.V. reads *"first trusted,"* the margin reads "hoped." The actual word used is *proelpizo*, to "fore-hope." Of this prior hope the Spirit is the seal, and as such is *"the holy Spirit of promise."*

What promise is in view? There is but one promise in the Prison Epistles. The Gentiles who formed the church of the One Body were by nature *"aliens from the commonwealth of Israel, and strangers from the covenants of promise"* (Ephesians 2:12), but through grace they became, *fellow-heirs, and of the same Body, and partakers of His promise in Christ by the gospel; whereof I (Paul) was made a minister* (Ephesians 3:6-7).

This promise takes us back to the period of Ephesians 1:4,

*before the foundation of the world, according to the promise of life, which is in Christ Jesus ... according to His own purpose and grace, which was given us in Christ Jesus, before age-times* (II Timothy 1:1, 9).

The realization of this unique promise is described by the Apostle in Colossians 3:

*When Christ, Who is our life, shall appear, then shall you also appear with Him in glory* (Colossians 3:4).[4]

## Parousia and Epiphany

Believing as we do that all Scripture is given by inspiration of God, we must be careful to distinguish between the different words used by God when speaking of the hope of His people. We observe that the word *parousia* **usually translated** *"coming,"* is found in such passages as the following:

*What shall be the sign of Thy COMING [parousia] and of the end of the age?* (Matthew 24:3).

*The COMING [parousia] of the Lord* (I Thessalonians 4:15).

---

4. [*Editor:*] For more information on the hope (or expectation) of the Body of Christ, see:
   - *Hope*, Charles H. Welch, Part 1 – *Bible Student's Notebook* #493; Part 2 – *Bible Student's Notebook* #494; Part 3 – *Bible Student's Notebook* #495;
   - *"The Hope of Israel" vs. "That Blessed Hope,"* Clyde L. Pilkington, Jr., *Bible Student's Notebook* #485;
   - *The Timing and Nature of Our Hope*, Clyde L. Pilkington, Jr., *Bible Student's Notebook* #510;
   - *The Hope of Paul's Prison Epistles*, Tom Ballinger, *Bible Student's Notebook* #582.

# Chapter 4 – The Hope of the Third Sphere

*The COMING [parousia] of our Lord Jesus Christ* (II Thessalonians 2:1).

*They that are Christ's at His COMING [parousia]* (I Corinthians 15:23).

*The COMING [parousia] of the Lord draweth nigh* (James 5:8).

*The promise of His COMING [parousia]* (II Peter 3:4).

*Not ashamed before Him at His COMING [parousia]* (I John 2:28).

*Parousia* is used to describe the hope of the church during the period when *"the hope of Israel"* was still in view. Consequently we find it used in the Gospel of Matthew, by Peter, James and John, ministers of the circumcision, and by Paul in those epistles written before the dispensational change of Acts 28.

A different word is used in the Prison Epistles. There, the word *parousia* is never used of the Lord's coming or of the hope of the church, but the word *epiphany*. In I Thessalonians 4 the Lord descends from heaven; in II Thessalonians 1 He is to be revealed from Heaven. This is very different from being manifested *"in glory,"* i.e., where Christ now sits *"on the right hand of God."*

While, therefore, the hope before all other companies of the redeemed is *"the Lord's coming,"* the *"prior-hope"* of the church of the Mystery is rather *their going* to be *"manifested with Him in glory."*[5]

---

5. [*Editor:*] For studies on the *three spheres*, see:
   - *The Three Spheres of Future Glory*, Dr. E.W. Bullinger, <u>Bible Student's Notebook 596;</u>
   - *The Three Spheres: Distinguishing Between Them*, H. W. Fry, <u>Bible Student's Notebook #613;</u>
   - *The Hope of the Third Sphere: Manifestation in Glory*, Charles H. Welch, *Bible Student's Notebook*.

# Chapter 5

## The 3 Dispensational "Hopes" of the 3 Spheres of Glory

*by* — Charles H. Welch (1880-1967)

*O*nly one Greek word and its compounds are translated *"hope,"* these words are *elpizo,* to hope, to hope for; *proelpizo,* to hope before; *apelpizo,* to hope for again; *elpizomenoi,* things hoped for; *elpis,* hope.

No other word in the English language can be suggested as a better rendering of *elpis* than "hope," and yet all have to acknowledge that, in common use, hope has degenerated in its meaning. We can speak of a forlorn hope, or sometimes a person who has no grounds for hope at all will say "I hope so." "Expectation is a conviction that excludes doubt," and this is the temper of the word *elpis.* When we use the word "hope" we must remember to keep it on the ground of confident expectancy, not merely hoping for the "possible" but confidently expecting the fulfillment of a promise.

Where we read of *"hope"* in the New Testament, we often find in the context a reference either to a "promise" or to a "calling." For example, Paul before Agrippa says,

> *Now I stand and am judged for **the hope of the promise** made of God unto our fathers; unto **which promise our twelve tribes,** instantly serving God day and night, hope to come* (Acts 26:6-7).

Here there is no possibility of making a mistake. Not only is the hope that is in view the fulfillment of a promise, but it is the fulfillment of

*51*

a specific promise *"made of God unto our fathers."* Further, there is no ambiguity as to those who entertain this hope; the words *"our twelve tribes"* are too explicit to permit of spiritualizing. Other examples will occur to the reader, and will come before us in the prosecution of our present study. For the moment it is sufficient that the principle should be clear, that *hope looks to the fulfillment of a promise.* It is therefore necessary to discover what promise has been made to any particular company before we can speak with understanding of their hope. Another prerequisite is a knowledge of the "calling" concerned.

> *That ye may know what is* **the hope of His calling** (Ephesians 1:18).

> *Even as ye are called in* **one hope of your calling** (4:4).

The realization of our hope in the future will be in agreement with our calling now by faith.

> *Now faith is the substance of things* **hoped** *for* (Hebrews 11:1).

Recent discoveries among the papyri of Egypt have brought to light the fact that the word "substance" was used in New Testament times to signify the "Title Deeds" of a property. Every believer holds the title deeds now, by faith, the earnest and first-fruits of the inheritance that will be entered when his hope is realized. As every believer does not necessarily belong to the same calling, and most believers grant a distinction between "Kingdom" and "Church," while some realize the further distinction between "Bride" and "Body," it follows that the character of the calling must be settled before the hope can be defined.

## THREE SPHERES OF BLESSING

There are at least three distinct spheres of blessing indicated in the New Testament:

## The Earth

*Blessed are the meek; for they shall inherit the earth* (Matthew 5:5).

## The Heavenly City

*The city of the living God, the heavenly Jerusalem ... and church of the firstborn, which are written in heaven* (Hebrews 12:22-23).

## Far Above All

*He ascended up, far above all heavens* (Ephesians 4:10).

*And made us sit together in heavenly places* (2:6).

These three spheres of blessing correspond to three distinct callings:

## The Kingdom

*Thy kingdom come, Thy will be done in earth ...* (Matthew 6:10).

## The Bride

*The Bride, the Lamb's wife ... the holy Jerusalem, descending out of heaven from God* (Revelation 21:9-10).

## The Body

*His body ... the church: whereof I [Paul] am made a minister, according to the dispensation of God which is given to me for you ... the mystery which hath been hid from ages and from generations* (Colossians 1:24-26).

These three spheres of blessing, each with its special calling, have associated with them three groups of people in the New Testament. The first sphere of blessing is exclusive to **Israel** according to the flesh; the second to believers from among both "**Jew** and **Greek**," while in the third sphere the calling is addressed to "**you Gentiles**."

### Israel According to the Flesh

*My kinsmen according to the flesh, who are Israelites; to whom pertaineth the adoption, and the glory, and the covenants, and the giving of the law, and the service of God, and the promises, whose are the fathers, and of whom as concerning the flesh Christ came, Who is over all ...* (Romans 9:3-5).

### Abraham's Seed
(Includes believing Gentiles)

*Having begun in the Spirit, are ye now made perfect by the flesh? ... they which are of faith, the same are the children of Abraham. ... For as many of you as have been baptized into Christ, have put on Christ. There is neither Jew or Greek ... for ye are all one in Christ Jesus. And if ye be Christ's, then are ye Abraham's seed, and heirs according to the promise* (Galatians 3:3, 7, 9, 27-29).

### The One New Man

*That He might create in Himself of the twain one new man, so making peace* (Ephesians 2:15, RV).

The limits of this article will not permit of extensive proofs of the suggestions made in the foregoing paragraphs, or of a detailed exposition of the passages concerned; but we believe that the matter is sufficiently clear for us to go forward with our inquiry.

Seeing, then, that there are three spheres of *blessing*, with their three associated *callings*, we should expect to find three phases of the "Coming" of the Lord.

Chapter 5 – The 3 Dispensational "Hopes" of the 3 Spheres of Glory

## THE HOPE OF THE FIRST SPHERE

*The Sign of the coming of the Son of Man*

The earthly ministry of the Lord Jesus Christ was limited to the people of Israel, and had special regard to the promise made to David concerning Israel's King. It also had in view the promise made to Abraham concerning the blessing of all of the families of the earth, but did not, at that time, extend to them, being concentrated rather on Israel from whom, as the appointed channel, the blessing should flow to all nations.

We shall now bring scriptural proof of these statements, and then proceed to show that Matthew 24-25 speak of *the hope of Israel,* and that this phase of the Second Advent has nothing to do with the hope of the Body of Christ.

### Proof that the Earthly Ministry Was Limited in the First Instance to Israel

*Now I say that Jesus Christ was a minister of the **circumcision** for the truth of God, to confirm the promises made unto the fathers* (Romans 15:8).

*Go not into the way of the Gentiles, and into any city of the Samaritans enter ye not; but go rather to the lost sheep of the house of **Israel*** (Matthew 10:5-6).

*I am not sent but unto the lost sheep of the house of ISRAEL* (Matthew 15:24).

### Proof that the Promise Made to David Concerning a King was in View

*Where is He that is born KING of the Jews? ... in Bethlehem* (Matthew 2:2-5).

*Tell ye the daughter of Zion, "Behold, thy KING cometh unto thee"* (Matthew 21:5).

*"What think ye of Christ, whose Son is He?" They say unto Him, "The Son of DAVID"* (Matthew 22:42).

*David ... being a prophet, and knowing that God had sworn with an oath to him, that of the fruit of his loins, according to the flesh, HE WOULD RAISE UP CHRIST TO SIT ON HIS THRONE; He seeing this before, spake of the resurrection of Christ* (Acts 2:30-31).

**Proof that the Promise to Abraham Concerning Israel as the Chosen Channel of Blessing to the Gentiles Was in View**

*Ye are the children of the prophets, and of the covenant which God made with our fathers, saying unto Abraham, "And in thy seed shall all the kindreds of the earth be blessed." UNTO YOU FIRST God, having raised up His Son Jesus, sent Him to bless YOU, in turning away every one of you from his iniquities* (Acts 3:25-26).

The consideration of these Scriptures in their setting provides sufficient proof for the statements made concerning the character of the Savior's earthly ministry.

We are now in a position to consider Matthew 24-25, which is a prophecy of the Second Coming of Christ, and concerns the Hope of Israel as distinct from the Hope of the Body of Christ.

The threefold prophecy of the coming of the Lord as revealed in Matthew 24 was given in answer to the threefold question of the disciples.

- *When shall these things be?*
- *What shall be the sign of Thy coming?*
- *And the end of the world* [age]*?*

The evidence which follows sufficiently shows that, in this passage, the Hope of Israel and not the Hope of *"the church which is His Body"* is the subject.

### Three Proofs that Matthew 24 Speaks of the Hope of Israel

First, the Greek word translated "end" is *sunteleia*, a word at that time well known to every Jew, for it was the name of the third great feast, namely *"the feast of ingathering, which is in the end of the year"* (Exodus 23:16). This is evidence that Israel's hope is in view.

Second, we find that this coming of the Lord is to be preceded by *"wars and rumours of wars."* Because of the fact that there have been, and yet will be, many wars and rumours of wars since the setting aside of Israel, these words, as they stand, cannot be construed as evidence that Israel's Hope is in view. If, however, we turn to the Old Testament origin of the reference, *"For nation shall rise against nation, and kingdom against kingdom"* (Matthew 24:7), we shall see that it comes from Isaiah's prophetic *"Burden of Egypt"* (Isaiah 19:1-2), the passage ending with the words,

> *Blessed be Egypt My people, and Assyria the work of My hands, and Israel Mine inheritance* (Isaiah 19:25).

This reference, therefore, when seen in the light of its Old Testament setting, gives further evidence for the fact that Israel is in view in Matthew 24.

Third, this coming of the Lord takes place after the prophetic statements of Daniel 9:27 and 12:11 have been fulfilled.

> *When ye therefore shall see the abomination of desolation, spoken of by Daniel the prophet, stand in the holy place ... then shall be great tribulation ... IMMEDIATELY AFTER THE TRIBULATION of those days ... shall appear the sign of the Son of man in heaven ... and they shall see the Son of man COMING IN THE CLOUDS OF HEAVEN* (Matthew 24:15-30).

As the detailed exposition of this chapter is not our purpose, and as these three items provide proof beyond dispute that the Second Coming of Christ as here made known cannot be the hope of the Body of Christ, we feel that no unbiased reader will desire further delay in prosecuting our inquiry.

## The Hope of the Second Sphere

*The Acts and Epistles of the Period*

We must now turn our attention to the evidence of Scripture as to the character of the Hope during the period covered by the Acts of the Apostles. Some commentators on this book appear to forget that it is the record of the "Acts" of the Apostles, and had no existence until those "Acts" were accomplished. If the founding of the church at Corinth chronicled in Acts 18 is an act of the apostle Paul, both Crispus (:8) and Sosthenes (:17) being mentioned by name, then the epistle written by the same apostle to the same church, again mentioning Crispus and Sosthenes by name, must be included as the Divine complement of the record of Acts 18.

The aspect of the Hope in view in the Acts and in the epistles written during that period to the churches founded by the Apostles must of necessity be the same. Any attempt to make the ministry of Paul during the Acts differ from the epistles of the same period is false, and must be rejected. There can be no doubt that the Hope entertained by the churches during the period covered by the Acts of the Apostles was a phase of the Hope of Israel. This will, we trust, be made clear to the reader by the quotations and comments given hereafter.

> When they therefore were come together, they asked of Him, saying, "Lord, wilt Thou at this time restore again the kingdom to Israel?" (Acts 1:6).

This question arose after the forty days' instruction given by the risen Christ to His disciples, during which time He not only opened the

Scriptures, but *"their understanding"* also (Luke 24:45).

> *Repent ... and He shall send Jesus Christ, Which before was preached unto you: Whom the heaven must receive until the times of restitution of all things, which God hath spoken by the mouth of all His holy prophets since the world began. ... Ye are the children of the prophets. ... Unto you first ...* (Acts 3:19-26).

These words of Peter, spoken after Pentecost, cannot be separated from the hope of Israel without violence to the inspired words. It may be that some readers will interpose the thought, "These are from the testimony of Peter; what we want is the testimony of Paul." We therefore give two more extracts from the Acts, quoting this time from the ministry of Paul.

> *And now I stand and am judged for the hope of the promise made of God unto our fathers: unto which promise our twelve tribes, instantly serving God day and night, hope to come* (Acts 26:6-7).

> *Paul called the chief of the Jews together ... "because that for the hope of Israel I am bound with this chain"* (Acts 28:17, 20).

Not until the Jewish people were set aside in Acts 28:25-29 does Paul become *"the prisoner of Jesus Christ for you Gentiles."* Until it was a settled fact that Israel would not repent and that the promise of Acts 3:19-26 would be postponed, the Hope of Israel persisted and all of the churches that had been brought into being up to that time were of necessity associated with that Hope. See the testimony of Romans, which is set out in much fuller detail after the reference to the heavenly calling is completed.

### The Heavenly Calling

We must pause for a moment here to remind the reader that Abraham stands at the head of two companies: an earthly people, the great nation of Israel; and a heavenly people, associated with the *heavenly phase* of God's promise to Abraham, and made up of the believing remnant of Israel and believing Gentiles. This heavenly side of the Abrahamic promise is referred to by the Apostle in Hebrews and Galatians:

> *He looked for a city ... They seek a country. ... They desire a better country, that is, an heavenly; wherefore God is not ashamed to be called their God: for He hath prepared for them a city* (Hebrews 11:10, 14, 16).

> *If ye be Christ's, then are ye Abraham's seed, and heirs according to the promise. ... Jerusalem which is above is free, which is the mother of us all* (Galatians 3:29, 4:26).

This *heavenly calling* of the Abrahamic promise constitutes the Bride of the Lamb, as distinct from the restored Wife which refers to Israel as a nation. We leave the reader to verify these statements for himself by referring to Isaiah, Jeremiah and Hosea, where Israel's restoration is spoken of under the figure of the restored Wife; and to the Book of the Revelation where the heavenly city is described as the Bride. During the time of the Acts of the Apostles, the churches founded by Paul were *"Abraham's seed, and heirs according to the promise"* (Galatians 3:29). The Apostle speaks of *"espousing them to one husband, that I may present you as a chaste virgin to Christ"* (II Corinthians 11:2).

This heavenly phase of the Hope of Israel was the hope of all of the churches established during the Acts, until Israel was set aside as recorded in Acts 28.

## The Testimony of Romans

The epistles written by Paul before his imprisonment were Galatians, Hebrews, Romans, I and II Thessalonians, and I and II Corinthians. We are sure that any well-instructed reader, who was asked to choose

## Chapter 5 – The 3 Dispensational "Hopes" of the 3 Spheres of Glory

from this set of epistles the one giving the most recent as well as the most fundamental teaching of the apostle for this period, would unhesitatingly choose the epistle to the Romans.

In this epistle we have the solid rock foundation of justification by faith, where *"no difference"* can be tolerated between Jew and Gentile. When, however, we leave the sphere of doctrine (Romans 1-8), and enter the sphere of dispensational privileges, we discover that differences between Jewish and Gentile believers remain.

The Gentile, who was justified by faith, was nevertheless reminded that he was at that time in the position of a wild olive, grafted into the true olive tree, from which some of the branches had been broken off through unbelief. The grafting of the Gentile into Israel's olive tree was intended (speaking after the manner of men) to provoke Israel to jealousy. When, in the days to come, these broken branches shall be restored, *"All Israel shall be saved."*

These statements from Romans 11 are sufficient to prevent us from assuming that, because there is evidently DOCTRINAL equality in the Acts period, there is also DISPENSATIONAL equality. This is not so, for Romans declares that the Jew is still *"first,"* and the middle wall still stands, making membership of the One Body as revealed in Ephesians impossible.

In Romans 15 we have a definite statement concerning the hope entertained by the church at Rome. Before quoting the passage, Romans 15:12-13, we would advise the reader that the Greek word rendered *"trust"* in :12 is *elpizo,* and the word *"hope"* in :13 is *elpis.* There is also the emphatic article *"the"* before the word *"hope"* in :12. Bearing these points in mind, we can now examine the hope entertained by the church at Rome as ministered to by Paul before his imprisonment.

> *There shall be a Root of Jesse, and He that shall rise to reign over the Gentiles; in Him shall the Gentiles hope. Now the God of*

*that hope fill you with all joy and peace in believing, that ye may abound in hope, through the power of the Holy Spirit* (Romans 15:12-13).

Here we are on firm ground. Paul himself teaches the church to look for the millennial kingdom and for the Savior as the *"Root of Jesse"* Who shall *"reign over the Gentiles."* How can this hope be severed from *"the Hope of Israel"*? How can it be associated with the *"Mystery"* which knows nothing of Abraham, or of Israel, but goes back before the *"foundation of the world,"* and reaches up to heavenly places? In case the reader should be uncertain of Paul's references to the millennial Kingdom, we quote from Isaiah 11:

*And there shall come forth a rod out of the stem of Jesse. ... He shall smite the earth with the rod of His mouth, and with the breath of His lips shall He slay the wicked. ... The wolf also shall dwell with the lamb. ... And in that day there shall be a Root of Jesse, which shall stand for an ensign of the people; to It shall the Gentiles seek: and His rest shall be glorious* (:1, 4, 6, 10).

The reader should consult the note on Isaiah 11:4 given in *The Companion Bible*, where the reading, *"He shall smite the oppressor"* (*ariz*) is preferred to the A.V. *"He shall smite the earth"* (*erez*). This reading establishes a link with II Thessalonians 2:8,

*And then shall that Wicked be revealed, whom the Lord shall consume with the spirit of His mouth, and shall destroy with the brightness of His coming.*

Before referring to I Thessalonians 4, which presents the hope of the church *at that time* very clearly, we must say something about the strange avoidance of the second epistle that so many manifest when dealing with this subject.

# Chapter 5 – The 3 Dispensational "Hopes" of the 3 Spheres of Glory

## The Importance of a Second Epistle to the Thessalonians

If a business man were to treat his correspondence in the way that some believers treat the epistles of Paul, the results would be disastrous. A second letter, purporting to rectify a misunderstanding arising out of a previous letter, would, if anything, be more important and more decisive than the first; yet there are those whose system of interpretation demands that they shall claim I Thessalonians 4 as the revelation of their hope, who nevertheless either neglect the testimony of II Thessalonians or explain it away as of some future mystical company unknown to the Apostle. Let us first verify that these two epistles form a definite pair, written by the same writer, at the same period, to the same people, about the same subject.

### Identity of Address

FIRST EPISTLE

*Paul, and Silvanus, and Timotheus, unto the church of the Thessalonians which is in God the Father and in the Lord Jesus Christ* (1:1).

SECOND EPISTLE

*Paul, and Silvanus, and Timotheus, unto the church of the Thessalonians in God our Father and the Lord Jesus Christ* (1:1).

### Identity of Theme

FIRST EPISTLE

*Remembering without ceasing your work of faith, and labor of love, and patience of hope in our Lord Jesus Christ, in the sight of God and our Father* (1:3).

*The coming of our Lord Jesus Christ with all His saints* (3:13).

## Second Epistle

> *We are bound to thank God always for you, brethren, as it is meet; because that your faith groweth exceedingly, and the love of every one of you all towards each other aboundeth; so that we ... glory ... in your patience* (1:3).

> *The Lord Jesus shall be revealed from heaven with His mighty angels, in flaming fire* (1:7-8).

### The Special Purpose of Second Thessalonians

The Thessalonian Church had been disturbed by the circulation of a letter purporting to have come from the Apostle, and by certain messages given by those who claimed to have "the spirit." These messages distorted the Apostle's teaching concerning the coming of the Lord, as taught in the church while he was with them and mentioned in the 4th chapter of his letter.

> *We beseech you, brethren ... that ye be not soon shaken in mind or be troubled, neither by spirit, nor by word, nor by letter as from us, as that the day of Christ* [or the Lord] *is at hand. Let no man deceive you by any means: for that day shall not come, except there come a falling away first* (2:1-3).

Before the hope of the church at Thessalonica could be realized, certain important prophecies awaited fulfillment. As we have seen, the hope during the period of the Acts (and therefore that of I Thessalonians 4) was essentially the Hope of Israel. When I Thessalonians 4 was written, Israel was still God's people. The Temple still stood, and the possibility (speaking humanly) of Israel's repentance had still to be reckoned with.

If the Hope of Israel was about to be fulfilled, then Daniel 9-12 must be fulfilled also, together with many other prophecies of the time of the end. This we have seen to have been the testimony of the Lord

# Chapter 5 – The 3 Dispensational "Hopes" of the 3 Spheres of Glory

Himself in Matthew 24, and so far Israel had not been set aside (*i.e.*, when the epistles to the Thessalonians were written).

The following predicted events must precede the coming of the Lord as revealed in I and II Thessalonians:

- The apostasy must come first (*"falling away,"* Greek, *apostasia*).

- The Man of Sin must be revealed in the Temple (the word *"Temple"* is the same as in Matthew 23:16).

- The coming of this Wicked One will be preceded by a satanic travesty of Pentecostal gifts. (The same words are used as of Pentecost, with the addition of the word "lying.")

- This Wicked One shall be *"consumed"* and *"destroyed"* with the brightness of the Lord's coming (see Isaiah 11:4).

*All of this* the Apostle had told the Thessalonian church when he was with them, before he wrote I Thessalonians 4 (see II Thessalonians 2:5).

The Thessalonians had already been taught by the Apostle himself concerning the events of prophecy, and would doubtless have read I Thessalonians 4 in harmony with his teaching had they not been deceived by false interpretations. The reference to the Archangel would have taken them back to Daniel 10-12. The epistle of Jude uses exactly the same word as is used here, and tells us that the Archangel's name is Michael (Jude 9).

Immediately following the great prophecy of the seventy weeks, with its climax in the *"Abomination of desolation,"* we have the revelation of Daniel 10. There the veil is partially withdrawn, and a glimpse is given of the satanic forces behind the *"powers that be."* Michael is said to be [Israel's] *"your Prince"* and in Daniel twelve we read,

> *And at that time shall Michael stand up, the great prince which standeth for the children of Thy people: and there shall be a time of trouble, such as never was since there was a nation ... and many of them that sleep in the dust of the earth shall awake* (Daniel 12:1-2).

Here we have Michael identified with the people of Israel, and when he stands up the great tribulation and the resurrection take place. *This follows the events of Daniel 11,* which are briefly summarized in II Thessalonians 2. Compare, for example, the following passages:

> *He shall exalt himself, and magnify himself above every god, and shall speak marvelous things against the God of gods* (Daniel 11:36).

> *Who opposeth and exalteth himself above all that is called God, or that is worshipped* (II Thessalonians 2:4).

## I and II Thessalonians and Revelation 13

If the reader would read consecutively Daniel 9-12, I Thessalonians 4-5, II Thessalonians 1-2, and Revelation 13, the testimony of the truth itself would be so strong as to need no human advocate.

Our space is limited, and we therefore earnestly ask all who value the teaching of the Scriptures regarding *"that Blessed Hope"* to read and compare these portions most carefully and prayerfully. When this is done, let the question be answered, "What have all these Scriptures to do with the church of the dispensation of the Mystery, a church called into being consequent upon Israel's removal and the suspension of Israel's hope?" The answer can be only that, while the close association of the hope of the Thessalonians with the hope of Israel was consistent with the character of the dispensation then in force, the attempt to link the *"one hope of our calling"* with prophetic times is a dispensational anachronism and a failure to distinguish things that differ.

## "Till He Come"

The coming of the Lord referred to in I Corinthians 11:26 must be the same hope as was entertained by the Thessalonians, and by the church at Rome (Romans 15:12-13). The Apostle himself summarizes this hope in Acts 28:20 as the *"Hope of Israel."*

The Corinthian epistle deals with a variety of subjects, and is addressed to different sections of the church. Some called themselves by the name of Paul, others by the name of Cephas. Some were troubled with regard to the question of marriage, and others with regard to deportment questions.

The section in which the words *"till He come"* occur is addressed to those whose *"fathers"* were *"baptized unto Moses"* (I Corinthians 10:1); whereas the section that immediately follows is addressed to Gentiles (12:2). Concerning the question of marriage, the Apostle writes,

> *I suppose therefore that this is good for the present distress. ... The time is short: it remaineth, that both they that have wives be as though they had none; and they that weep, as though they wept not. ... and they that buy, as though they possessed not* (I Corinthians 7:26-30).

Shall we fall into the error of teaching, as some have taught, that marriage is wrong because of what Paul says in this chapter? If we do, what shall we say of his wonderful words concerning husband and wife in Ephesians 5? Or of his advice that the younger women should not only marry, but marry again if left as widows (I Timothy 5:9-14)?

The right interpretation is clearly that Paul's advice in I Corinthians 7 was true *at the time,* because the Second Coming of Christ was expected to take place during the lifetime of some of his hearers. He speaks as he does *"because of the present necessity,"* and because *"the time is short."* When writing to the Thessalonians, he rightly identifies himself with the imminent hope of the Lord's coming by saying, "*We which are alive*" (I Thessalonians 4).

The *"present necessity"* of I Corinthians 7 is no longer applicable on account of the failure of Israel and the suspension of their Hope.

So in I Corinthians 11, the teaching of the chapter was true only while the hope of that calling was still imminent. When the people of Israel passed into their present condition of blindness, as they did in Acts 28, their hope passed with them, not to be revived until the end of the days, when the Apocalypse is fulfilled.

Meanwhile a new dispensation has come in, a dispensation associated with a *"mystery"* and unconnected with Israel. In the very nature of things a change of dispensation means a change of calling. It introduces a new sphere and a fresh set of promises, and demands a re-statement of its own peculiar hope.

## Hope of the Third Sphere

*The Manifestation in Glory*

Before considering the special characteristics of the Hope of the One Body, it may be of service to set out some of the distinctive features of the *Dispensation of the Mystery*, so that, perceiving the unique character of its calling, we shall be compelled to believe the unique character of its Hope.

### Special Features of the Present Dispensation

First of all, let us observe two features that marked the previous dispensation, but are now absent.

(1) The Presence and Prominence of Israel

The testimony of the Gospels (Matthew 10:6; 15:24), the witness of

# Chapter 5 – The 3 Dispensational "Hopes" of the 3 Spheres of Glory

Peter (Acts 3:25-26), and the testimony of Paul (Romans 1:16; 3:29; 9:1-5; 11:24-25; 15:8), all combine to show that the nation of Israel was an important factor in the outworking of the purpose of the ages, and that during the period covered by the Gospels and the Acts, no blessing could be enjoyed by a Gentile in independence of Israel. It is evident that, with the setting aside of this favored people, a change in dispensation was necessitated.

(2) The Presence and Prominence of Miraculous Gifts

Throughout the public ministry of the Lord Jesus, and from Pentecost in Acts 2 until the shipwreck on the island of Melita in Acts 28, supernatural signs, wonders and miracles accompanied and confirmed the preached Word. Not only did the Lord Himself and also His apostles work miracles, but during the time of the Acts ordinary members of the church were in possession of spiritual gifts in such abundance that they had to seek the Apostle's advice as to their regulation in the assembly (I Corinthians 14:26-40).

The miracles of Mark 16, Acts 2 and I Corinthians 12-14 are not the experience of the church of today. Their absence, together with the setting aside of the people of Israel, constitute two pieces of negative evidence in favor of a new dispensation.

We are not, however, limited to negative evidence. Scripture also provides definite evidence of a positive kind, which we must now consider.

### The Prison Ministry of the Apostle Paul

When Paul spoke to the elders of the church at Ephesus, he made it quite plain that one ministry was coming to an end and another, which would be closely associated with prison, was about to begin. He reviewed his past services among them, and told them among other things that they should see his face no more (Acts 20:17-38). Later, before King Agrippa, he reveals the important fact that when he was converted and commissioned by the Lord in Acts 9, he had been told that at some subsequent time the Lord would appear to him again and give him a second commission (Acts 26:15-18).

## The Dispensational Boundary of Acts 28

Right up to the last chapter of the Acts, Israel and miraculous gifts continued to occupy their pre-eminent place (Acts 28:1-10, 17, 20). Upon his arrival at Rome, Paul, although desirous of visiting the church (Romans 1:11-13), sent first for the *"chief of the Jews,"* telling them that *"for the Hope of Israel"* he was bound with a chain. After spending a whole day with these men of Israel, seeking unsuccessfully to persuade them *"concerning Jesus"* out of the law and the prophets, he finally pronounces their present doom of blindness, adding,

> *Be it known therefore unto you, that the salvation of God is sent unto the Gentiles, and that they will hear it* (Acts 28:28).

During the two years of imprisonment that followed, the Apostle ministered to all who came to him, teaching those things which *"concern the Lord Jesus Christ"* with no reference this time either to the law or to the prophets (Acts 28:30-31).

## The Present Dispensation a New Revelation

The omission of *"the law and the prophets"* from Acts 28:31, as compared with :23, is an important point. Throughout the early ministry of the Apostle he makes continual and repeated appeal to the Old Testament Scriptures; but when one examines the "Prison Epistles," one is struck by the absence of quotation.

The reason for this change is that Paul, as the prisoner of Jesus Christ for the Gentiles, received the Mystery *"by revelation"* (Ephesians 3:1-3). This mystery had been hidden from ages and generations, until the time came for Paul to be made its minister (Colossians 1:24-27). It could not, therefore, be found in the Old Testament Scriptures.

## Two Special Features of this New Calling

- Chosen: *"before the foundation of the world"* (Ephesians 1:4) and *"before age-times"* (II Timothy 1:9).

- Sphere of Blessing: *"in heavenly places, far above all principality and power. ... seated together in heavenly places in Christ Jesus"* (Ephesians 1:3, 20-21; 2:6).

## The Prison Epistles

While the very nature of things demands a new dispensation consequent upon Israel's removal, we are not left to mere inference. There is a definite section of the New Testament with special teaching relating to the present dispensation. This is found in the epistles written by Paul as the prisoner of the Lord for us Gentiles. These epistles are five in number, but we generally refer to the "four Prison Epistles," as that to Philemon is practical and personal and makes no contribution to the new teaching.

The four Prison Epistles are:

EPHESIANS

*The Dispensation of the Mystery*
Basic Truth

PHILIPPIANS

*The Prize*
Outworking

COLOSSIANS

*The Dispensation of the Mystery*
Basic Truth

II Timothy

*The Crown
Outworking*

The reader will find evidence in each of these epistles that they were written from prison and that they form part of the ministry referred to in Acts 28:31.

## The New Phase of Hope Necessitates Prayer

While prayer should accompany the Word at all times, there is no need to pray for "revelation" concerning one's hope if it is already revealed. Words can be scarcely clearer than those employed in I Thessalonians 4, and if this chapter still represented the present hope for the One Body, there would be no need for the Apostle to speak as he does in Ephesians 1. In :17, he prays that the saints might receive,

> *the spirit of wisdom and revelation in the knowledge of Him ... that ye may know what is the hope of His calling* (Ephesians 1:17-18).

It might be well if the reader pondered the marginal reading of Ephesians 1:17 where, instead of *"in the knowledge of Him,"* we read, *"for the acknowledging of Him."*

This raises a most important point. Many fail to go forward with the truth, not because of inability to understand the meaning of plain terms, but because of failure to *"acknowledge Him."* The Apostle pauses in his teaching to tell his hearers that, before another step can be taken, acknowledgment of what has already been revealed must be made. To acknowledge the truth of the Mystery is to put oneself out of favor with denominationalism, and many a child of God who says, "I do not see it," is really making a confession of failure to acknowledge the revelation of truth connected with the ascended Lord.

## This New Phase of Hope Associated with a New Promise

Hope and promise are necessarily linked together. Promises that were the basis of expectation during the Acts were the promises *"made unto the fathers."* Now the fathers had no promises made to them concerning heavenly places *"where Christ sitteth at the right hand of God."* The promises made to the fathers never extended beyond "the Bride" or "the Heavenly Jerusalem," but in Ephesians we have a sphere *"far above all."*

In Ephesians 1:12, where the A.V. reads *"first trusted,"* the margin reads *"hoped;"* and as we cannot speak of *"the blessed trust"* or *"the trust of the second coming,"* it is best to keep to the translation *"hope."* The actual word used is *proelpizo*, to "fore-hope." Of this *prior hope* the Holy Spirit is the seal, and as such is *"the Holy Spirit of promise"* (:13).

What promise is in view? This promise takes us back to the period of Ephesians 1:4, *"before the foundation of the world"*:

> *According to the promise of life, which is in Christ Jesus ... according to His own purpose and grace, which was given us in Christ Jesus, before age-times* (II Timothy 1:1, 9).

It is this one unique promise that will be realized when the *Blessed Hope* is fulfilled. Its realization is described by the Apostle in Colossians 3:

> *When Christ, Who is our life, shall appear, then shall ye also appear with Him in glory* (Colossians 3:4).

We are waiting for *"Christ our life,"* and so awaiting *"the promise of life,"* which is our Hope. The word *"appearing"* might be translated *"manifestation,"* and will be familiar to most readers in the term "epiphany."

## *Parousia* and Epiphany

Believing as we do that all Scripture is given by inspiration of God, we must be careful to distinguish between the different words used by God when speaking of the Hope of His people. We observe that the word *parousia,* usually translated *"coming,"* is found in such passages as the following:

> *What shall be the sign of Thy COMING and of the end of the age?* (Matthew 24:3).
>
> *The COMING of the Lord* (I Thessalonians 4:15).
>
> *The COMING of our Lord Jesus Christ* (II Thessalonians 2:1).
>
> *They that are Christ's at His COMING* (I Corinthians 15:23).
>
> *The COMING of the Lord draweth nigh* (James 5:8).
>
> *The promise of His COMING* (II Peter 3:4).
>
> *Not ashamed before Him at His COMING* (I John 2:28).

This word is used to describe the Hope of the church *during the period* when *"the Hope of Israel"* was still in view. Consequently we find it used in the Gospel of Matthew, by Peter, James and John, ministers of the circumcision, and by Paul in those epistles written before the dispensational change of Acts 28.

A different word is used in the Prison Epistles. There, the word *parousia* is never used of the Hope of the Body of Christ, but the word *epiphany.* In I Thessalonians 4 the Lord descends from heaven; in II Thessalonians 1 He is to be revealed from heaven. This is very different from being manifested *"in glory,"* i.e., where Christ now sits *"on the right hand of God."*

# Chapter 5 – The 3 Dispensational "Hopes" of the 3 Spheres of Glory

While, therefore, the Hope before all other companies of the redeemed is *"the Lord's Coming,"* our "prior-hope" is rather to be *"manifested with Him in glory."*

While the epistle to Titus is not a "Prison Epistle," it belongs to the same group as I and II Timothy. There, too, we read that we should live,

> *Looking for that Blessed Hope, and the manifestation of the glory of our great God and Savior Jesus Christ* (Titus 2:13).

### The Marriage of the King's Son

We may perhaps illustrate these different aspects of the Second Advent by using the occasion of the marriage of the King's son at Westminster Abbey. The marriage is one, whether witnessed in the Abbey itself, from a grandstand, or from the public footway. So, whatever our calling, the hope is one in this respect, that it is Christ Himself. Nevertheless, we cannot conceive of anyone denying that to be permitted to be present in the Abbey itself is something different from sitting in a grandstand until the King's son, accompanied by "shout" and "trumpet," descends from the Abbey to be met by the waiting people. These waiting people outside of the Abbey form one great company, although differentiated as to point of view.

So the *early church,* together with the Kingdom saints, form one great company, although some, like Abraham, belong to *"the heavenly calling"* connected with Jerusalem that is above, while others belong to the Kingdom which is to be *"on earth."*

We can hardly believe that any subject of the King would *prefer* the grandstand over the closer association of the Abbey itself; and we can hardly believe that any redeemed child of God would "prefer" to wait on earth for the descent of the Lord from heaven if the *"manifestation with Him in glory"* were a possible hope before him. We cannot, however, force these things upon the heart and conscience.

We can only respond to the exhortation to be,

> *ready always to give an answer to every man that asketh you a reason of the hope that is in you with meekness and reverence* (I Peter 3:15).

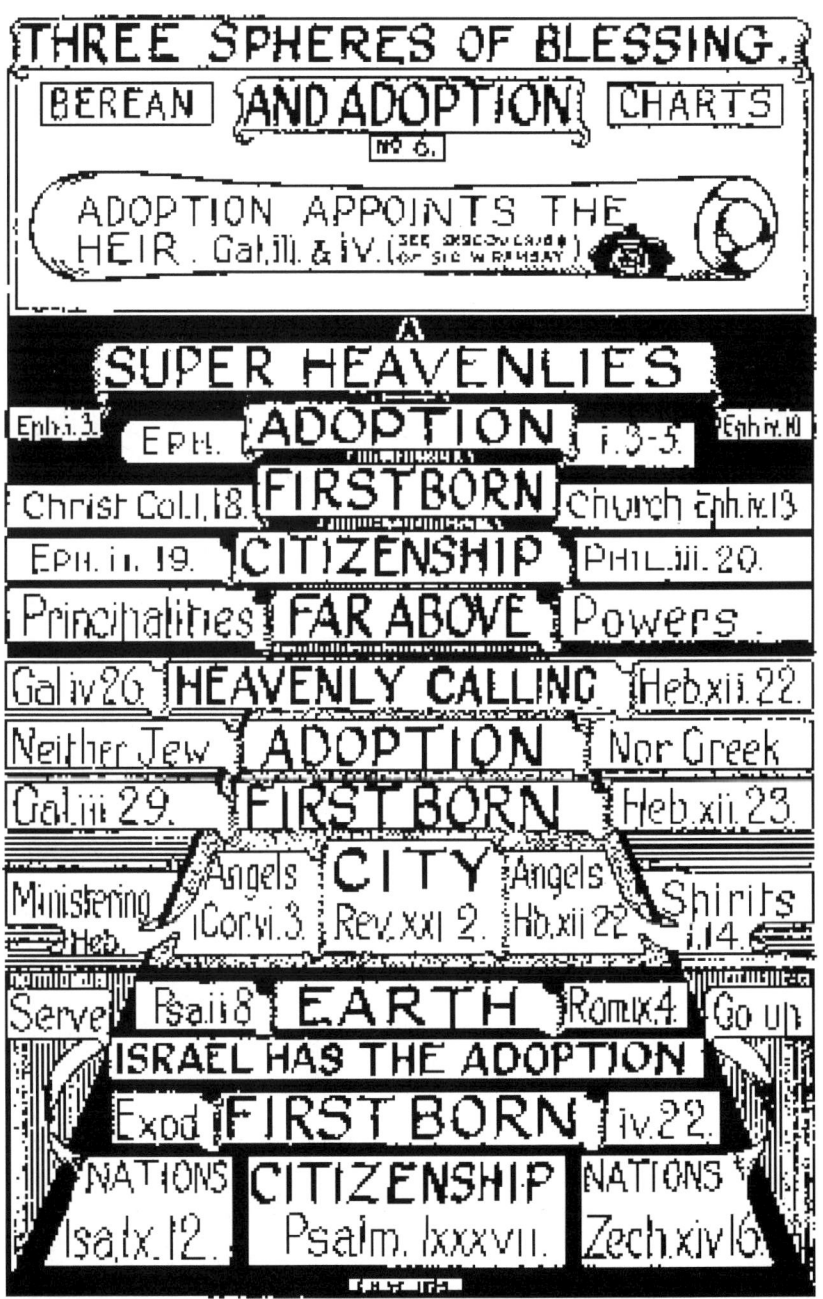

# Your Part

Now that you have read this book, it's your turn.

If the truths presented here have helped you, don't let these truths die in your hands.

Please write to us and let us know your thoughts concerning its content.

Consider assisting us in getting this book into the hands of those who would be encouraged and strengthened by its message:

- Recommend it to your friends and loved ones.

- Order additional copies to give as gifts.

- Keep extra copies on hand to loan to others.

If you have not read the author's other works, order them today.

We would be honored to have your fellowship in getting this book freely to those who hunger spiritually. We have daily opportunities to send it to pastors, Sunday school teachers, Bible college professors and students, Bible class teachers, and prisoners.

# Do You Subscribe to the
# Bible Student's Notebook™?

This is a periodical that ...
- Promotes the study of the Bible.
- Encourages the growth of the believer in grace.
- Supports the role of the family patriarch.
- Is dedicated to the recovery of truth that has too long been hidden under the veils of traditionalism, prejudice, misunderstanding and fear.
- Is not connected with any "Movement," "Organization," "Mission," or separate body of believers, but is sent forth to and for all saints.

The *Bible Student's Notebook*™ is a *free* electronic publication published semi-weekly (100 times a year).

## SUBSCRIBE TODAY!
To receive your *free* electronic subscription, email us at:
bsn@studyshelf.com

*Bible Student's Notebook*™
PO Box 265 Windber, PA 15963
*www.BibleStudentsNotebook.com*
*1-800-784-6010*

# DAILY EMAIL GOODIES™

Do you receive our
*Daily Email Goodies™?*

These are free daily emails that contain short quotes, articles, and studies on Biblical themes.

These are the original writings of Clyde L. Pilkington, Jr, as well as gleanings from other authors.

<u>Here is what our readers are saying</u>:

"Profound! Comforting! Calming! Wonderful!" – NC

"The Daily Email Goodies continue to bless my heart! ... They provide plenty of food for thought." – IL

"I really appreciate the Goodies!" – VA

"Your Daily Email Goodies are making me aware of authors whose names I don't even know." – GA

"I am glad to be getting the Daily Email Goodies – keep 'em coming." – IN

Request to be added to our free
*Daily Email Goodies*™

If you would like to be added to the mailing list, email us at:

<u>Goodies@StudyShelf.com</u>

# Enjoy Books?
## Visit us at:
## www.StudyShelf.com

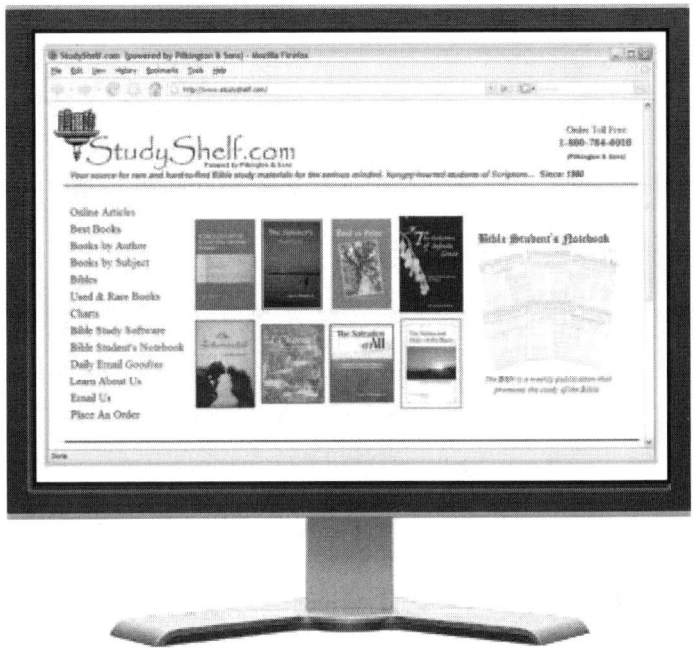

Over the years we have often been asked to recommend books. The requests come from believers who longed for material with substance. Study Shelf™ is a collection of books which are, in our opinion, the very best in print. Many of these books are "unknown" to the members of the Body of Christ at large, and most are not available at your local "Christian" bookstore.

## YOU CAN:
### *Read*
A wealth of articles from past issues of the *Bible Student's Notebook* ™

### *Purchase*
Rare and hard to find books, booklets, leaflets, Bibles, etc. in our 24/7 online store.